For Gwen Burrows and Geoff Woodward

OXFORD
UNIVERSITY PRESS

Great Clarendon Street, Oxford OX2 6DP

Oxford University Press is a department of the University of Oxford.
It furthers the University's objective of excellence in research, scholarship,
and education by publishing worldwide in

Oxford New York

Athens Auckland Bangkok Bogotá Buenos Aires Calcutta
Cape Town Chennai Dar es Salaam Delhi Florence Hong Kong Istanbul
Karachi Kuala Lumpur Madrid Melbourne Mexico City Mumbai
Nairobi Paris São Paulo Singapore Taipei Tokyo Toronto Warsaw

with associated companies in Berlin Ibadan

Oxford is a registered trade mark of Oxford University Press
in the UK and in certain other countries

British Library Cataloguing in Publication Data available

ISBN 0 19 276217 6

Printed in Hong Kong

THE PHANTOM'S
FANG–TASTIC SHOW

horror poems to haunt
your days and . . . nights

WRITTEN BY **WES MAGEE**
ILLUSTRATED BY **LEO BROADLEY**

OXFORD
UNIVERSITY PRESS

Contents

J
827

And Finally

To Begin at the Beginning

Imprisoned in this book of verse
are Ghoul and Gremlin, Ghost . . . and worse.
To loose the Horrors from their cage . . .

just turn the page.

The Phantom's Fang-tastic Show

The Phantom says,
'Roll up! Roll up for Spectres!
Roll up for Apparitions!
Come in and see the Gremlins
—all sizes, shapes, conditions.
To see my Show to best effect
put on these weirdo 3-D specs
from "Spec-ter-al Opticians"!'

The Phantom says,
'Roll up! Roll up for Werewolves!
See dopey Doppelgängers!
Come in and watch my Hellcats
mud-wrestling with Headbangers!
In order to protect your lugs
make sure you wear these ear-hole plugs
when Draculas drop clangers!'

The Phantom says,
'Roll up! Roll up for Ghosties!
See Demons disembowelling!
You must not miss the Mummy
seal-wrapped in ancient towelling!
You'll need to don this steel-lined hat
as things go Whizz! Crash! Wallop! Splat!
when Poltergeists are prowling!'

The Phantom says,
'Roll up! Roll up for Zombies!
Watch nifty Necromancers!
My whacky whistling Wizards
are fabulous entrancers!
You'll nod your head and tap your feet
to spooky band—"The Banshee Beat".
You'll *love* the UnDead-Dancers!'

'So,
Roll up for my Fang-tastic Show!
Be quick, we're starting in a mo.
Come in and view a creepy cast.
The last few seats are filling fast.
Make haste!
There is no time to spare.
Please take your places
. . . if you dare!'

The Phantom says . . .

To seek out spooks and sprites we should
explore a dank and dripping **Wood**.
If haunted glades you wish to see

just follow me.

The Woodsman and the Green Children

(Forest of Dean, 1857)

Masked by the forest's leafy screen
a Woodsman saw the strangest scene.
He gazed upon a dappled glade
and watched two children, coloured green.

He watched as on all fours they played
and loped like wolves from light to shade.
Amazed at how they snarled and yowled,
hid in the holt the Woodsman stayed.

Then came a she-wolf, sharp-fang jowled.
Into the dappled glade she prowled.
The Woodsman saw the children quail,
then run towards her when she growled.

The poor man felt his courage fail
and, as the two green children howled,
he hastened down the forest trail,
returned to town and told this tale,
returned to town and told this tale.

The Wraiths of Wilderness Wood

Dripping and dank
and chill as stone
Wilderness Wood
is overgrown,
its creatures gone,
its birds flown.

Deep in ancient Wilderness Wood
    there lies a swamp, a stagnant bog,
its peaty ooze no longer home
    to crested newt or common frog.
Just sphagnum moss and fungi live
    on fallen branch and rotting log.

More than six centuries ago
    poor pilgrims stopped off at this Wood.
They gorged on berries, herbs, and nuts;
    one gathered acorns in his hood.
Then ventured deeper, laughing loud,
    until before the swamp they stood.

For fun they tore down spiders' webs
    which hung from boughs like veils of lace,
then grabbed at gauzy dragonflies.
    Excitement flushed each pilgrim's face.
But when they stepped into the swamp
    they sank . . . and vanished without trace.

That was the eighth day of July,
　　and on that date each year, they say,
the pilgrims' wraiths rise from the swamp
　　and for release they wail and pray.
Scared by these ghosts all creatures fled.
　　In fear the birds flew far away.

　　　　　Dripping and dank
　　　　　and chill as stone
　　　　　Wilderness Wood
　　　　　is overgrown,
　　　　　its creatures gone,
　　　　　its birds flown.

Today, as I explore the Wood,
　　there's utter silence all around,
and hacking through the nettles, briars,
　　my trainers squelch in soggy ground.
As ivy tendrils clutch my hair
　　I reach the swamp the pilgrims found.

On this, the eighth day of July,
　　I find a brambled thicket, hide,
and watch as from the stagnant swamp
　　the pilgrims' ghosts begin to rise.
Smoke-grey they writhe in ceaseless prayer
　　and scare me with their anguished cries.

All day the wretched pilgrims float.
　　For sweet release they plead and rave
until, at dusk, I watch the wraiths'
　　last ragged ectoplasmic wave.
Then one by one they slowly sink
　　back to their oozy, swampy grave.

In fear I quit my thicket hide
  and crash through brambles in a state.
Just like the creatures of the Wood
  I flee before it is too late,
and as cruel thorns snag jeans and shirt
  I leave the pilgrims to their fate,
    I leave the pilgrims to their fate.

Dripping and dank
and chill as stone
Wilderness Wood
is overgrown,
its creatures gone,
its birds flown . . .

The Game at the Phantom's Hallowe'en Party

(Held in Hanging Man's Wood)

'Let's play *Murder in the Dark*!'
the Phantom prattles out.
The party guests all punch the air.
'That's cool!' and 'Whoarr!' they shout.

Smack on the stroke of midnight
the game gets under way.
Murder is a deadly game
and everyone must play.

Around the Wood run witches,
their nails as sharp as knives.
Disgusting dirty demons
are bolting for their lives.

It's *Murder in the Dark*, Olé!
It is *the* party game to play.

Grey ghosts and ghouls and goblins
jump up and screech like trains.
A skeleton in irons
starts rattling her chains.

Bogles hide in hollow oaks.
Two zombies—Zak and Zond—
trip up on a rotten log
and splash into the pond.

A terrible, blood-freezing shriek
comes slicing through the night.
'The Murderer's d . . . d . . . done his work!'
a wizard squeaks with fright.

It's *Murder in the Dark*, Olé!
It is *the* party game to play.

A werewolf howls his heart out.
The Horrid Hulk tramps by.
There's blood upon his boots
and *Murder* in his eye.

An owl is hooting, 'Is It You?'
until gnarled Gremlin Grimm
identifies the Hulk and croaks,
'The Murderer . . . it's him!'

'Caught you! Caught you!' chant the guests.
They boo the Horrid Hulk
who sticks out his spotty tongue
and stomps off in a sulk.

It's *Murder in the Dark*, Olé!
It is *the* party game to play.

Hulk crashes through the briars and ferns
and vanishes from sight.
The Phantom says, 'Game over!
Buzz off, you lot. Goodnight.'

The Phantom gives a massive yawn
and slopes off to his bed.
The Wood returns to silence.
Full moon glides overhead.

There'll be a party here next year
and for a laugh and lark
why don't *you* turn up and play
Murder in the Dark?

Tawny Owl

Hoo Hoo
Hoo-oo-oo-oo
a haunting cry.
To feed the owlets
a creature must die . . .

A tawny owl wrapped in its brown feather cloak
is perched on the branch of an ancient oak.
Slowly it blinks in the moon's gelid glow
as it watches the woodland floor far below.
Its night-sight vision can spot in the dew
a foraging mouse or a scavenging shrew.

Hoo Hoo
Hoo-oo-oo-oo
a haunting cry.
To feed the owlets
a creature must die . . .

The tawny owl's poised with razor-sharp beak
for the faintest rustle, movement, or squeak.
It silently swoops in the dead-of-night chill,
curved talons grasp, and the owl makes a kill.
Ghost-like it glides through the wood with its prey,
Now owlets can eat in the squirrels' old drey.

Hoo Hoo
Hoo-oo-oo-oo
a haunting cry.
To feed the owlets
a creature must die . . .

Spice Girl's Song

'Here in my cottage
deep in the green wood
I live on my own
and eat children pud.
No one would guess
that I'm up to no good
here in my cottage
deep in the green wood.

'I stand at the door
and look pretty nice.
My lipstick is red,
my eyes green as ice,
and my cottage is made
of sugar and spice
with caramel cats
and marzipan mice.

'Kids lost in the wood
stop off here to eat.
My windows and walls
they find such a treat.
They think that I'm ace
and terribly sweet
when I ask them inside
to rest their poor feet.

'As soon as they're trapped
I bolt the front door.
The shocked kids see bones
all over the floor.
They see I'm a witch
with warts on my jaw,
one broken brown tooth
and wig made of straw.

'The kids try to hide
in my smelly old room
but I soon sniff them out
in the cobwebby gloom.
I give them a whack
with a dirty great broom
and into my oven
they go to their doom.

'I bake the lost kids
till they're tender and nice
then serve them up hot
with lashings of rice.
I garnish with gnats
and finely-ground lice
here in my cottage
of (hah!) sugar and spice.

'Parents come searching
—just as they should,
but none of them guess
I'm up to no good
or that their lost kids
are yum scrummy pud
here in my cottage
deep in the green wood.'

The Phantom says . . .

Here's a **Graveyard** with lichened stones
and ancient tombs and scattered bones.
There beyond the ruined church

we'll make a search.

In the Misty, Murky Graveyard

In the misty, murky graveyard
  there's a midnight dance,
and in moonlight shaking skeletons
are twirling in a trance.
Linked arm in bony arm
they point and pitch and prance,
down there in the graveyard
  at the midnight dance.

In the misty, murky graveyard
  there's a midnight rave,
and a score of swaying skeletons
are lurching round a grave.
Their toe bones tip and tap
and their rattling fingers wave,
down there in the graveyard
  at the midnight rave.

In the misty, murky graveyard
  there's a midnight romp,
and the squad of skinless skeletons
all quiver as they stomp.
To the whistle of the wind
they clink and clank and clomp,
down there in the graveyard
  at the midnight romp.

The Tomb near the Sea
(A true tale)

If you go to the west coast of Ireland
    seek the ruined church near the sea
and visit the thistle-thronged graveyard
    with its single lightning-struck tree.

Find the ivy-clad tomb lost in nettles
    —the one with slab fallen aside.
Kneel and prepare yourself for a shock
    as you peer to see what's inside.

In that tomb you'll spot rotting old coffins
    and hotchpotch of scattered dry bones.
You will sniff a rank mustiness rising
    from the shrouds, the soil, and the stones.

As your eyesight adjusts to the darkness
    you'll slowly discern in the gloom
a row of cracked skulls arranged on a ledge:
    ten skulls at the rear of the tomb!

Those cracked skulls have been there for decades
    but who they were no one can say,
for the names carved in the tomb's lichened slab
    have long since eroded away.

If you go to the west coast of Ireland
    seek that tomb and lightning-struck tree
that both stand in the thistle-thronged graveyard
    of the ruined church near the sea.

Cemetery Epitaphs

Here lies
Acker Abercrombie.
Crazy name.
Crazy zombie.
Slightly scary,
rather rude,
he walks at midnight
in the nude.

Two halves of Tracey Trump lie here.
She reached her eighty-seventh year.

She lived through floods and two World Wars.
Got sliced in automatic doors.

R.   I.   P.
   Here resteth
Werewolf Walter Witz
who chewed relations
   into bits
Aunts and uncles,
nephews, nieces
all ended up

Ripped In Pieces

'Please mark my grave
with just one flower.'
That was the wish
of Cynthia Tower.
So when she died
they raised a plinth
and marked upon it
        'Hiya, Cynth'.

Reserve this plot
    for Wes Magee,
convicted for
    bad poetree.
The judge declared
    his verse a crime,
and now Magee
    is doing rhyme.

R.I.P.

The Girl in the Graveyard

In early spring she's seen
flitting through the graveyard, tresses flowing.
She shelters from an April shower
in the lee of a mossed stone wall,
and is startled
when pigeons rise from the church tower
and flap away into the blue.
      But who is she, who?

          Why she comes
          and where she goes
          no one knows
          no one knows.

Barefoot in summer she's seen
treading between the tombstones
as the tower clock dully strikes one.
Swallows describe perfect arcs
in the insect-laden air
as she seeks shade from July's sun
beneath the dark foliage of a yew.
      But who is she, who?

          Why she comes
          and where she goes
          no one knows
          no one knows.

In September she's seen
kneeling beside an unmarked grave,
a red rose clutched in her hand.
Leaves spiral down
as rooks caw and circle above the elms.
When thunder rumbles across the land
she departs leaving footprints in the dew.
    But who is she, who?

        Why she comes
        and where she goes
        no one knows
        no one knows.

Shawled in December she's seen
slipping through the lych-gate
as heavy snow falls.
A robin's perched on a leaning headstone
as she waits, shivering,
beside the church tower's icy walls
perhaps recalling someone she once knew.
    But who is she, who?

        Why she comes
        and where she goes
        no one knows
        no one knows.

The Phantom says . . .

We'll flush out **Ghosts** in cobwebbed halls
and **Ghosts** that walk through solid walls.
Let's get the 'spook search' underway

without delay.

Up in the Attic . . .

something's glaring . . .
something's gurgling
something's staring
something's stirring
and
in the dark
in the dust
boxed Christmas lights
big tooth from a shark
sad rocking horse
a model Noah's Ark
cobwebby comics
doll's house painted green
dusty wine bottles
a bust of the Queen
leather-bound books
old sewing machine
Up in the attic

. . . And Down in the Cellar

Down in the cellar
  brown boot in a box
      remains of a cot
two brass mantel clocks
    buckets and brushes
      and musty old socks
          damp pile of coal
        a splintered pine door
              rusty rat trap
      and a snaggle-toothed saw
            six mildewy blankets
                  piled on the
                    stone floor
                        and
              something's moving
              something's moaning
                something's gawping
                  something's groaning . . .

The Ghosts of 'The Grange'

Miss Starvelling-Stamper died in 'twenty-four.
They found her stone-cold on the flagstoned floor.

She lay beside the kitchen's cast-iron range,
last Starvelling-Stamper to dwell at 'The Grange'.

Since then the mansion's been abandoned, locked:
its windows smashed, roof collapsed, sewers blocked.

The croquet lawn's been lost to Queen Anne's lace.
'The Grange' is now a sad, forgotten place.

Yet, nightly, ghosts creep from each crumbling wall
and gather in the leaf-strewn marble hall

—a chambermaid drifts up the woodwormed stairs,
a skivvy flicks at cobwebs on the chairs,

two snooty butlers wait where moonbeams slant,
see there a grim and gaunt tiaraed aunt.

Miss Starvelling-Stamper's ghost—last of the line—
lifts to her lips a goblet of French wine

and floats above the kitchen's flagstoned floor
where she was found stone-cold in 'twenty-four.

The Chimney Boy's Story
(His spirit speaks)

'Inside the chimney, high I climb.
It's dark inside the sooty stack.
I bang my head and graze my back.
I lose all sense of passing time.
Inside the chimney,
          high I climb.

'Inside the chimney, high I climb.
Far, far above . . . a patch of blue
where one white cloud drifts into view.
I stop to rest, but that's a crime.
Inside the chimney,
          high I climb.

'Inside the chimney, high I climb.
My bare feet slip on crumbling bricks.
I clear rooks' nests—dead leaves and sticks.
The Master yells, "Get working, brat!"
I'm starved. Sometimes I eat stewed rat.
Soot's in my hair. I'm tasting grime.
Inside the chimney,
          high I climb.'

Pauline the Poltergeist

At 'Creepy Cottage' something's up.
    On the hall mat there's a smashed cup,
and with the ashes in the grate
    lie fragments of a dinner plate.
Sharp knives and spoons are on the floor
    and someone's chucked an apple core.
Who, *who's* been throwing pans and bowls?
    And *who's* been flinging crusty rolls?

At midnight there's a dreadful noise
    as someone hurls the children's toys.
Whizz! and Whoosh! And Clang and Crash!
    Thud! and Thump! and Slam and Smash!
It's Pauline Poltergeist, a shade,
    who years ago worked as a maid
and now's returned to haunt each room
    and throw things with a Bash! Bang! Boom!

At 'Creepy Cottage' every day
    they try to scare the shade away
by playing tapes of Status Quo,
    but Pauline Poltergeist won't go.
She keeps on slinging antique jugs
    and lobbing snazzy coffee mugs.
Zip! and Zap! and Ping and Plop!
    Maid Pauline Poltergeist won't stop.

CREEPY HOLLOW

When Pauline bunged the Christmas pud
   the 'Cottage' people left for good.
They packed their bags without delay,
   jumped in their Jag and sped away.
Now 'Creepy Cott.' is up for sale
   but would-be buyers turn quite pale
when Pauline lets fly with a broom
   and sends them squealing from the room
      with a Whack! and a Wallop!
         and a Zonk! Zak! Zoom!

The Phantom says . . .

Terrible trolls and werewolves weird
—and tigers too—are rightly feared.
Where fact or fiction **Creatures** creep

we'll take a peep.

The Werewolf's Howl

There's a hideous,
horrible,
harrowing howl
and you know that a werewolf's
out on the prowl.
Stoke up the fire,
draw curtains tight,
lock all the doors
and keep out the night.
Don't give the werewolf
a chance to get in
for he's thirsty for blood
and hungry for skin.

The werewolf's a man
with fingernail claws,
hairs on his hands
and slavering jaws.
In anguish and pain
he rages and roars.
He's a werewolf at large in the dark,
in the dark.

The werewolf's a man
with red bloodshot eyes
who bays at the moon
in thunderclap skies.
His sharply fanged teeth
can deeply incise.
He's a werewolf at large in the dark,
in the dark.

The werewolf's a man
who's seeking a feast,
and only warm flesh
will appease the wild beast.
Those caught in his grip
all end up deceased.
He's a werewolf at large in the dark,
in the dark.

There's a hideous,
horrible,
harrowing howl
and you know that a werewolf's
out on the prowl.
Stoke up the fire,
draw curtains tight,
lock all the doors
and keep out the night.
Don't give the werewolf
a chance to get in
for he's thirsty for blood
and hungry for skin.

Tiger Might

Tiger,
a creature of contrasts.

Here, just asking to be stroked,
the velvety-soft striped fur coat.

There, the huge raised paw,
which can strike dead gazelle or goat.

Tiger,
a creature of contrasts.

Here, the glinting eyes,
two pools of shifting light.
    Tiger shine.
    Tiger bright.

There, the watchful beast,
fanged, lurking in shadows.
    Tiger fear.
    Tiger might.

In the Sixteenth Century
(An old woman speaks)

'I sit trussed with twine
on this vile ducking-stool
and I'm certain to drown
in the villagers' pool
for they say I bewitched
their root crops and oats,
crippled their children
and poisoned their goats.
The villagers say
I'm a witch and a drab,
they curse me and stone me
and call me Queen Mab.
They swear I cast spells
in my old cooking pot
and say I keep demons
and imps in my grot.
But I only have pets
like a frog and a bat,
a magpie, an adder,
and my lovely black cat.
I'm just an old woman
who lives in a grot
and I only make soup
in my old cooking pot.
I sit trussed with twine
while the villagers yell,
Duck the witch! Let her drown!
and *Send her to Hell!*
They cheer, oh, they cheer,
as the stool hurtles down
and into cold water
I plunge . . . and I drown . . .'

The Terrible Troll

There's a Terrible Troll
   down by the wild river.
Put one foot on his bridge
   and he'll bite out your liver.

He's a Terrible Troll,
   weird, wet-skinned, and warty.
He's as blue as a bruise
   and nastily naughty.

Oh, this Terrible Troll
   owns the humpyback bridge,
eats trespassers raw
   and keeps limbs in his fridge.

     He eats
   joggers and loggers
   and six-minute snoggers.
   Nippers and skippers
   and coach party trippers.
   Drivers and skivers
   and scuba-geared divers.
   Hikers and strikers
   and Hell's Angels bikers.

     He eats
   rappers and yappers
   and bash-yer-nose scrappers.
   Shoppers and boppers
   and 'What's this 'ere?' coppers.
   Jokers and stokers
   and girls wearing chokers.
   Runners and sunners
   and big blondie stunners.

And he gobbles
dirty dogs,
  mouse-munching mogs,
   fatso dads
    and layabout lads.
Grey old grans,
  Oasis fans,
   sleepy slobs
    and ya-booing yobs.
Lager louts,
  toggled sea scouts,
   mountainous mums,
    tramps, vagrants, and bums.

Yes, the Terrible Troll
  lives by the wild river.
Put one foot on his bridge
  and he'll bite out your liver.

Oh, the Terrible Troll
  is hairless and haughty.
His age, so I'm told,
  is two hundred and forty.

He's a Terrible Troll.
  He's a cruncher and squeezer.
Patellas and thigh bones
  he stores in his freezer.

      Remember this . . .

if you step on his bridge
you'll end up in his fridge.

The Phantom says . . .

In **School** scared pupils shed a tear
and teachers can engender fear.
In classrooms where wild rumours fly

we'll snoop and pry.

The Beast in the Boiler House

There's a huddle on the playground,
dozen pupils—maybe more,
all ear-wigging John-Paul's story
about what he heard and saw
when he ventured down the stone steps
to the Boiler House's door.

'I found an old key in the lock.
It was really thick with rust
and when the door creaked open,
wow, a t'rific pong of must!
I stepped inside and saw the place
was carpeted with dust.'

John-Paul paused
and scratched his nose.
'What happened next?'
asked Rachel Rose.
   And
      the huddled heads
         drew
            closer . . .

'The Boiler House was dark and hot.
My heart went boom-de-boom
when I heard the huge machinery
throb-throbbing in the gloom.
And then . . . I saw a "thing" arise
like a zombie from its tomb!'

John-Paul stopped
and tugged his ear.
'What happened next?'
breathed Bully Beer.
　　And
　　　　the huddled heads
　　　　　　drew
　　　　　　　　closer,
　　　　　　　　　　closer . . .

'A huge Beast lumbered forward.
Around its head buzzed flies.
Its matted fur coat crawled with lice
and it had three bloodshot eyes.
It reached out with a warty hand
to grab my arm. No lies!'

　　John-Paul coughed
　　and itched his chin.
　　'What happened next?'
　　gasped Tracey Thin.
　　　　And
　　　　　　the huddled heads
　　　　　　　　drew
　　　　　　　　　　closer,
　　　　　　　　　　　　closer,
　　　　　　　　　　　　　　closer . . .

'It gave a snarl. I turned and ran!
I heard it give a snotty sneeze.
I belted up the steep stone steps,
fell *there*, and grazed my knees.
I'm telling you, that scary Beast
would make your hot blood freeze!'

A bell rang.
The end of morning break.
'Some story, that,'
said Steven Steak.
  And
     the huddlers headed
       back to
        school.

And as they passed the steep stone steps
they stopped and gazed in awe
at the trace of blood where John-Paul fell,
then looking downwards saw
the old key really thick with rust
in the Boiler House's door . . .

The Strangest School Secretary

She's Queen Wasp of the Office
and her throne's a swivel chair.
Her fingernails are purple.
A wren nests in her hair.

Her eyes are green as seaweed
and she has a wildcat's glare.
She growls at timid teachers
just like a grizzly bear.

She makes inspectors nervous
and drives the parents spare.
Headmaster, can't you sack her?
You're right, he'd never dare!

Our secretary's the strangest.
She's really rather rare.
She's Queen Wasp of the Office
and her throne's a swivel chair.

Miss Drak: Blood Teacher

Miss Drak's on 'blood teacher' duty this week.
It's her job to staunch cuts and grazes.
The other teachers hate mopping-up blood
but Miss Drak's fervour amazes.

When you knock on the Staff Room door and gasp,
'Playground accident! It's Anne-Marie!'
Miss Drak leaps up and comes running at once.
On her face a look of sheer glee.

She licks her red lips and sets straight to work
dab dabbing blood from Anne-Marie's chin.
Awestruck we notice Miss Drak has two fangs
and a fiendishly devilish grin.

Rick's Revolting Rumours

At making rumours Rick's a master.
He dreams them up and spreads them faster
than any BBC newscaster.
    When, once, he spied a Schools' Inspector
    he said she was a ghost detector
    who'd come to seize a spooky spectre.

One of Rick's more revolting rumours
told of a Troll with scabs and tumours
who, in the toilets, showed pink bloomers.
    He put the Infants in a panic
    when spreading tales that Monsters manic
    had just arrived from the *Titanic*.

In Staff Room cages, Rick said, teachers
bred cockroaches and weirdo creatures
with red-rimmed eyes and vampire features.
    He whispered that caretaker Morgan
    was really a flesh-eating Gorgon
    who slurped behind the 'lectric organ.

Rick, with a grin, told little Mary
that in the Boiler Rooms it's scary.
Beware the Hag! he hissed. She's hairy!
    The Head, at lunch, was one fast gobbler.
    Rick said the cooks were out to nobble 'er
    by peppering the curry cobbler.

Rick's girl friend, Hannah, got the shivers
when told the canteen van delivers
intestines, eyeballs, lungs, and livers.
    The boy created one real chiller.
    He said Miss Take looked like Godzilla
    and that a zombie's out to k . . . ' . .

In class Rick's rumours cause a flutter.
'He's whacko!' some are heard to mutter,
while others mumble, 'What a nutter!'
    He spreads his stories thick as plaster,
    invents wild worlds of dire disaster.
    Rick's one cool rumours master-blaster.

The Phantom says . . .

Tall tales of **Buildings** new or old
can scare and make the blood run cold.
We'll open up each creaky door

and then explore.

In the Castle of Gloom

Oh, it's cold,
it's as cold as a tomb,
and it's dark
as a windowless room
in the Castle,
the Castle of Gloom.

    (Meet your doom,
       meet your doom,
          meet your doom . . .)

No sun through the shutters.
No candle flame gutters.
No log embers glimmer.
No silver plates shimmer.
  No lamps in the hall.
  No brands on the wall.
    No moonbeams at night.
   No starshine.
    No light.

Oh, it's cold,
it's as cold as a tomb,
and it's dark
as a windowless room
in the Castle,
the Castle of Gloom.

    (Meet your doom,
       meet your doom,
          meet your dooooooooooom . . .)

At the Deep Well . . .

*At the deep well, where young Jocelyn Joakes
climbed down the winding rope and fell
to his death in 1839.*

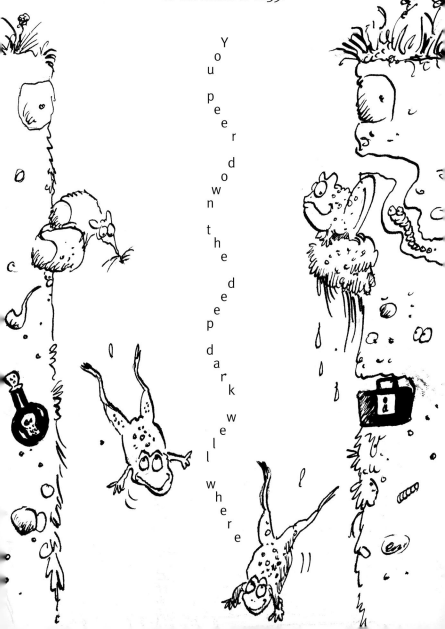

You
peer
down
the
deep
dark
well
where

54

t
h
e
r
o
p
e
s
n
a
p
p
e
d
a
n
d
J
o
c
e
l
y
n
f
e
l
l

Down here lies water,
icy cold,
its secret held
from days of old.
A faint voice echoes
far below;
a boy's last cry
from years ago.

From . . . Tina Queen's Diary

Monday, 9th December

Brr! It was cold today. Bitter!
We togged up and tramped across the field
where the Old Manor used to be.
Our boots left deep prints in the snow.
Jip (my dog) dug under an ancient oak
and rooted out a rusty oil lamp.
Dad reckoned it got buried there
when the Old Manor burned down a century ago.

Tuesday, 10th December

This morning I polished the oil lamp,
and did it shine? I'll say!
I placed it next to the clock radio
on the table beside my single bed.
Then something really weird happened.
The lamp seemed to glow
brighter and brighter,
and I got this strange feeling inside my head!

Wednesday, 11th December

Guess what? This morning I awoke
to find the oil lamp on the floor!
Somehow (but how?) it must have fallen
off my bedside table in the night.
Then, when I picked it up—wow!—
it felt *really* warm. Almost hot!
And it glowed brighter than ever.
You know, something about that lamp's not right . . .

Thursday, 12th December

Amazing! I suddenly woke at dawn
when the oil lamp clattered to the floor.
And *someone* was beside my bed.
There was *someone* standing there!
It was a girl, a ghostly girl
dressed like an old-fashioned maid.
She pointed a shimmering grey finger
at the lamp and shook her head. What a scare!

Friday, 13th December

Friday the 13th! Unlucky for me!
There was a fire in my bedroom at 3 a.m.
The smoke alarms went off,
and Dad rushed in to find my rug alight!
Yes, you've guessed it,
that wretched oil lamp had fallen again
only this time it was *red* hot!
It set my bedroom rug smouldering in the night!

Saturday, 14th December

That oil lamp is spooked, haunted.
Dad thinks it could have caused the fire
that burned down the Old Manor
a century ago. I reckon so.
I tramped across the field with Jip
and reburied the lamp under the ancient oak.
Now it's back where it belongs (thank goodness!),
out of harm's way deep beneath the snow!

The House on the Hill

It was built years ago
by someone quite manic
and sends those who go there
away in blind panic.
They tell tales of horrors
that can injure or kill,
designed by the madman
who lived on the Hill.

    If you visit the House on the Hill for a dare,
    remember my words . . . 'There are dangers. Beware!'

The piano's white teeth
when you plonk out a note
will bite off your fingers
and go for your throat.
The living room curtains
—long, heavy, and black—
will wrap you in cobwebs
if you're slow to stand back.

    If you enter the House on the Hill for a dare,
    remember my words . . . 'There are dangers. Beware!'

The fridge in the kitchen
has a self-closing door.
If it knocks you inside
then you're ice-cubes . . . for sure.
The steps to the cellar
are littered with bones,
and up from the darkness
drift creakings and groans.

    If you go to the House on the Hill for a dare,
    remember my words . . . 'There are dangers. Beware!'

Turn on the hot tap
and the bathroom will flood,
not with gallons of water
but litres of blood.
The rocking-chair's arms
can squeeze you to death:
a waste of time shouting
as you run . . . out . . . of . . . breath.

Don't say you weren't warned or told to take care
when you entered the House on the Hill . . . for a dare.

The Phantom says . . .

So closes my Fang-tastic Show.
It's time to let the horrors go.
My **Charm** will ward off things that bite

just for tonight.

The Phantom's Charm for Sweet Dreams

May the Ghost
   lie in its grave.
May the Vampire
   see the light.
May the Witch
   keep to her cave,
and the Spectre
   melt from sight.

May the Wraith
   stay in the Wood.
May the Banshee
   give no fright.
May the Ghoul
   begone for good,
and the Zombie
   haste its flight.

May the Troll
   no more be seen.
May the Werewolf
   lose its bite.
May all Spooks
   and Children Green
fade for ever
   in
      the
         night . . .

And Finally

The final spooky verse is penned.
The poems draw to their haunting end.
Permit yourself just one last look

then close the book.

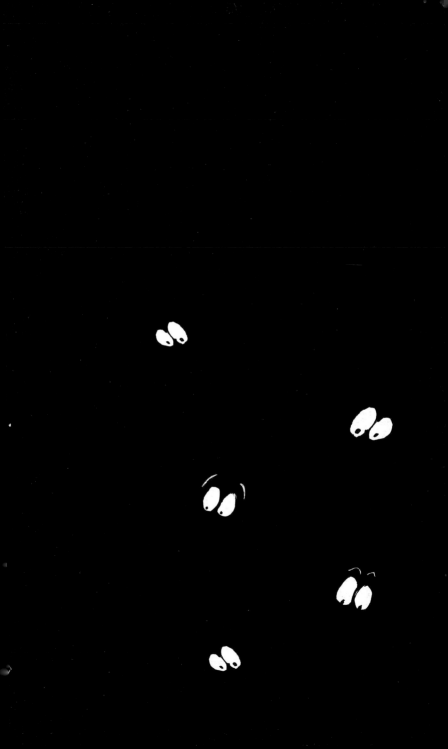